SO.EI / d/ddt / 80/0

Easy Cookbooks for Kids

Easy Breakfasts
From Around the World

Sheila Griffin Llanas

Enslow Elementary

Library of Congress Cataloging-in-Publication Data

Llanas, Sheila Griffin, 1958-
  Easy breakfasts from around the world / Sheila Griffin Llanas.
    p. cm. – (Easy cookbooks for kids)
  Includes index.
  ISBN 978-0-7660-3707-6
  1. Breakfasts--Juvenile literature. 2. International cooking--Juvenile literature. 3. Quick and easy cooking--Juvenile literature. 4. Cookbooks.
  I. Title.
    TX733.L59 2011
    641.5'2--dc22

2010039480

Paperback ISBN: 978-1-59845-269-3

Printed in China

052011 Leo Paper Group, Heshan City, Guandong, China

10 9 8 7 6 5 4 3 2 1

To Our Readers: We have done our best to make sure all Internet addresses in this book were active and appropriate when we went to press. However, the author and the publisher have no control over and assume no liability for the material available on those Internet sites or on other Web sites they may link to. Any comments or suggestions can be sent by e-mail to comments@enslow.com or to the address on the back cover.

Photo Credits: All photos are from Shutterstock.com, except as noted.
© John Ketola, p. 26 (pannukakku); © PIFood/Alamy, p. 23; © SoFood Collection/Photolibrary, p. 32 (fruit salad); © 1999 Artville, LLC, (all maps) pp. 15, 17, 20, 23, 26, 29, 32, 35, 38, 41, 44; © 2011 Photos.com, a division of Getty Images. All rights reserved., p.10 (mortar and pestle), p. 11 (vegetable peeler), p. 22 (pita), p. 33 (papaya); © Clipart.com., pp, 8, 9; © Nicole DiMella/ Enslow Publishers, Inc., p. 29 (kielbasa); © Noema Pérez, p. 20 (ful medames); © Photoalto/Pho- tolibrary, p.7; © Photolibrary, p. 35 (egg and toast); iStockphoto.com/© Don Nichols, p. 10 (cookie sheet); iStockphoto.com/© Linda & Colin McKie, p. 24 (ghee); p. 18 (pita); p. 31 (mustard); United States Department of Agriculture (USDA), p.14.

Cover Illustration: © 2011 Photos.com, a division of Getty Images. All rights reserved.

Warning: The recipes in this book contain ingredients to which people may be allergic, such as peanuts and milk.

Contents

Introduction

Every day, in countries around the world, people wake up and eat breakfast. What do you eat for breakfast? In the United States, cereal and toast with juice or milk are typical breakfast foods. In other cultures, people eat rice, soup, dried beans or vegetables for the first meal of the day. Breakfast can be healthy, delicious, and fun to eat. Have fun trying new flavors! Maybe you will find some new breakfast traditions.

As you use this cookbook, you will learn about countries around the world. Eleven recipes come from eleven countries or regions. When you follow a recipe, you can read about the country the dish comes from and the unique ingredients that flavor it.

Each recipe in this book has specific directions on WHAT YOU NEED and WHAT TO DO. You will also find cooking tips. The tips help you to be safe and have fun in the kitchen. They will make you a more skillful chef.

Be Safe!

Whenever you are in the kitchen, there are important safety rules to follow:

1. Always **ask a responsible adult** for permission to cook. Always have **an adult** by your side when you use the oven, the stove, knives, or any appliance.

2. If you have long hair, tie it back. Remove dangling jewelry and tuck in any loose clothing.

3. Always use pot holders or oven mitts when handling anything on the stove or in the oven.

4. Never rush while cutting ingredients. You don't want the knife to slip.

5. If you are cooking something in the oven, stay in the house. Always use a timer—and stay where you can hear it.

6. If you are cooking something on the stove, stay in the kitchen.

7. **ALLERGY ALERT!** If you are cooking for someone else, let them know what ingredients you are using. Some people have life-threatening allergies to such foods as peanuts, dairy products, and shellfish.

Cooking Tips and Tricks

Keeping Clean:

- Wash your hands before you start. Make sure to also wash your hands after touching raw poultry, meat, or seafood and cracking eggs. These ingredients may have harmful germs that can make you very sick. Wash knives and cutting boards with soap and water after they've touched these ingredients.

- Use two cutting boards (one for meat and one for everything else) to avoid getting any germs from the meat on other food.

- Rinse all fruits and vegetables under cool water before you use them.

- Make sure your work space is clean before you start.

- Clean up as you cook.

Planning Ahead:

- Read the recipe from beginning to end before you start cooking. Make sure that you have all the ingredients and tools you will need before you start.

- If you don't understand something in a recipe, ask an adult for help.

Measuring:

- To measure dry ingredients, such as flour and sugar, dip the correct size measuring cup into the ingredient until it is full. Then level off the top of the cup with the flat side of a butter knife. Brown sugar is the only dry ingredient that should be tightly packed into a measuring cup.

- To measure liquid ingredients, such as milk and oil, use a clear glass or plastic measuring cup. Make sure it is on a flat surface. Pour the liquid into the cup until it reaches the correct level. Check the measurement at eye level.

- Remember that measuring spoons come in different sizes. Be sure you are using a *teaspoon* if the recipe asks for it and not a *tablespoon*.

Mixing:

- Beat—Mix ingredients together *fast* with a wooden spoon, whisk, or an electric mixer.

- Mix—Blend ingredients together with a wooden spoon, an electric mixer, or a whisk.

- Stir—Combine ingredients together with a wooden or metal spoon.

Cooking Terms

Cooking has its own vocabulary. Here are some terms you should be familiar with:

bread (verb)—To coat or cover with a layer of flour or crumbs before cooking.

brown (verb)—To cook, usually in oil, until the food turns light brown.

chop—To cut into bite-sized pieces.

condiments—Food that add a flavorful accent to a dish, such as mustard and tartar sauce.

cube—To cut into small, cube-shaped pieces.

cuisine—The type of cooking used in a particular country or area.

dice—To cut into small pieces (smaller than chopped).

drizzle—To pour a small amount of liquid in a stream over a dish.

fry—To cook in hot fat in a pan on top of the stove.

garnish—A bit of colorful food, such as parsley, that adds flavor to a dish and makes it look more attractive.

grate—To shred into small pieces with a grater.

herbs—Plants such as oregano and basil, used to give food a distinctive flavor. They can be used fresh or dried.

marinate (verb)—To soak food in a dry rub or liquid blend of seasonings (a marinade) so that it absorbs the flavors and becoms more tender.

mince—To chop into tiny pieces.

sauté—To fry lightly in a small amount of oil or fat.

savory—Highly flavored and tasty; not sweet.

seasonings—Ingredients used to bring out the flavor of a food, such as salt, pepper, herbs, and spices.

simmer—To cook over low heat just below the boiling point.

spice—A seasoning that has a strong or spicy aroma, for example, cinnamon or pepper.

staple—A main food item, needed nearly every day, such as flour or milk.

Cooking Tools

baking dish

cutting board

cookie sheet

mortar and pestle

frying pan

oven mitt

measuring cups

paring knife

measuring spoons

pie pan

potato masher

strainer

rolling pin

rubber spatula

slotted spoon

spatula

whisk

soup pot

vegetable peeler

11

Nutrition

The best food is healthy as well as delicious. In planning meals, keep in mind the guidelines of the food pyramid:

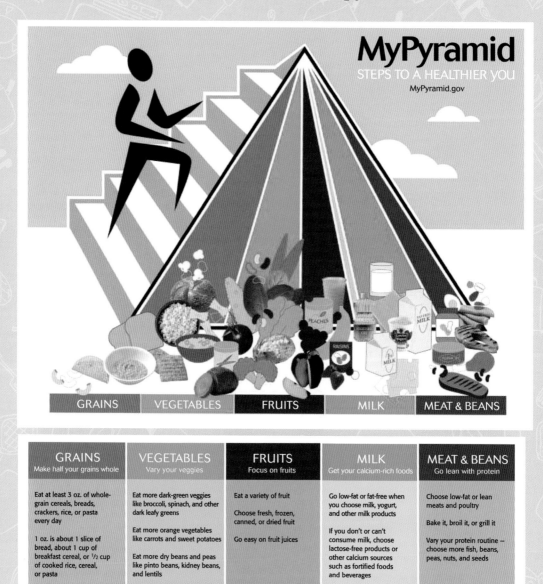

GRAINS	VEGETABLES	FRUITS	MILK	MEAT & BEANS
Make half your grains whole	Vary your veggies	Focus on fruits	Get your calcium-rich foods	Go lean with protein
Eat at least 3 oz. of whole-grain cereals, breads, crackers, rice, or pasta every day 1 oz. is about 1 slice of bread, about 1 cup of breakfast cereal, or ¹/₂ cup of cooked rice, cereal, or pasta	Eat more dark-green veggies like broccoli, spinach, and other dark leafy greens Eat more orange vegetables like carrots and sweet potatoes Eat more dry beans and peas like pinto beans, kidney beans, and lentils	Eat a variety of fruit Choose fresh, frozen, canned, or dried fruit Go easy on fruit juices	Go low-fat or fat-free when you choose milk, yogurt, and other milk products If you don't or can't consume milk, choose lactose-free products or other calcium sources such as fortified foods and beverages	Choose low-fat or lean meats and poultry Bake it, broil it, or grill it Vary your protein routine — choose more fish, beans, peas, nuts, and seeds
For a 2,000-calorie diet, you need the amounts below from each food group. To find the amounts that are right for you, go to MyPyramid.gov.				
Eat 6 oz. every day	Eat 2¹/₂ cups every day	Eat 2 cups every day	Get 3 cups every day; for kids aged 2 to 8, it's 2	Eat 5¹/₂ oz. every day

Conversions

Recipes list amounts needed. Sometimes you need to know what that amount equals in another measurement. And sometimes you may want to make twice as much (or half as much) as the recipe yields. This chart will help you.

DRY INGREDIENT MEASUREMENTS	
Measure	**Equivalent**
1 tablespoon	3 teaspoons
¼ cup	4 tablespoons
½ cup	8 tablespoons
1 cup	16 tablespoons
2 cups	1 pound
½ stick of butter	¼ cup
1 stick of butter	½ cup
2 sticks of butter	1 cup
LIQUID INGREDIENT MEASUREMENTS	
8 fluid ounces	1 cup
1 pint (16 ounces)	2 cups
1 quart (2 pints)	4 cups
1 gallon (4 quarts)	16 cups

This book does not use abbreviations for measurements, but many cookbooks do. Here's what they mean:

c—cup

oz.—ounce

lb.—pound

T or tbsp.—tablespoon

t or tsp.—teaspoon

Chapter 1

Brown Bread

with Honey-Molasses Butter

Weekend breakfasts in Turkey are large and fancy—cheese, olives, bread, hard-boiled eggs, and sausages. But on workdays, breakfast can be simple— bread with butter and honey, eaten with hot tea.

Turkey

Turkey is a Middle Eastern nation that lies both in Europe and Asia. About 3 percent of the country occupies the easternmost tip of southern Europe. To the east, the rest of Turkey covers a large, mountainous peninsula called Anatolia or Asia Minor.

Honey

Turkish farmers harvest a rare kind of honey. Black pine honey comes from the Turkish Pine tree. Aphids, very small insects, suck the tree sap and secrete sugar. Bees collect the sugar and make honey. Farmers gather the honey. Pine tree honey tastes strong and is as dark as molasses.

What You Need

Equipment:
Bowl

Mixing spoon

Toaster

Knife

Ingredients:
Sliced brown bread, like pumpernickel, rye or wheat

2 tablespoons butter

2 tablespoons honey

1 tablespoon molasses

What to Do

1. Let the butter soften to room temperature.
2. Measure butter, honey, and molasses in a bowl.
3. Cream the mix for 1–2 minutes.
4. Toast the brown bread.
5. Spread some honey butter on the toast.

Serves 2–4.

(1-2 slices of toast per person)

What's This?

Cream means to mix butter with sugar. Stir fast to make it a pale yellow color, and light and fluffy.

Cook's Tip

Taste. Add more honey or more butter to make your perfect blend. Eat it with your favorite juice, milk, or tea.

Cook's Tip

Store leftovers in the refrigerator for another day.

Chapter 2

Chorizo con Huevos

Chorizo(cho-REE-so) is a kind of pork sausage. The dish chorizo con huevos (cho-REE-so cone HWAY-vos) is fried chorizo and scrambled eggs. The mixture can be rolled into tortillas to make breakfast burritos.

Mexico

Mexico is the northernmost country of Latin America. No one can pinpoint the exact date or location for the invention of the tortilla. According to legend, tortillas were invented by a peasant for his hungry king in ancient times. The first tortillas, which date back to approximately 10,000 BC, were made of native corn.

17

Chorizo

Chorizo is sausage made from ground pork. Mexican chorizo is hot and spicy, made with chile peppers. Chiles give chorizo its dark orange color. (Spanish chorizo is sweeter, spiced with paprika and garlic.) Chorizo is soft when it cooks. Look for chorizo in the cooler section of the grocery store near bacon.

What You Need

Equipment:

Skillet (frying pan)

Chef's knife or scissors

Cooking spatula or wooden spoon

Bowl

Whisk or fork

Ingredients:

Chorizo

1–2 eggs per person

Tortillas

Garnish (optional):

Salsa (you can use store-bought) or pico de gallo; shredded cheddar cheese

Cook's Tip

Chorizo often comes raw in tubes. Fry as much as you want. Save the rest for another day.

What's This?

Salsa means sauce. *Pico de gallo* means "rooster's beak." It is fresh salsa made from chopped tomato, onion, and chili peppers.

What to Do

Fry the chorizo:

1. Heat a skillet on medium heat.
2. Slice the chorizo casing ◄······ open length-wise with a knife or scissors.
3. Scoop the meat into the hot skillet. Throw the casing away.
4. As the chorizo fries, break it up with your cooking spatula.
5. Stir the chorizo until it is cooked, about 7–8 minutes.
6. When sausage cooks, the fat separates from the meat. Drain the extra grease from the pan.

Scramble the eggs:

1. Crack the eggs into a bowl.
2. Beat the eggs with a fork or a whisk.
3. Pour the eggs over the chorizo in the pan.
4. Reduce heat to low.
5. Stir the scrambled eggs with the chorizo until they are cooked.
6. Serve on a plate with warm tortillas.
7. Taste before you add salt and pepper. Chorizo is really flavorful.

Serves as many people as you want

(1-2 eggs per person) For a treat, serve chorizo con huevos with cups of hot chocolate!

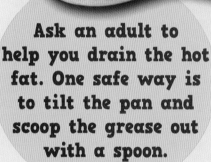

What's This?
Casing is the sausage covering that holds the meat together.

Cook's Tip

Ask an adult to help you drain the hot fat. One safe way is to tilt the pan and scoop the grease out with a spoon.

Cook's Tip

Some people like eggs moist and soft. Others like them dry and firm.

19

Chapter 3

Ful Medames

Ful medames (fool meh-DAHMS) is fava bean stew. It is often served with pita. **Ful** is the word for fava beans. **Medames** means "buried." Mashed, cooked fava beans are drizzled with olive oil, lemon juice, garlic, and other seasonings. Ful medames is simple, good food. It was once eaten mostly by hardworking peasant people. Today ful medames is prized as one of Egypt's national dishes.

Egypt

Egypt, a country in the Middle East, is home to one of the world's oldest civilizations. Many people travel to Egypt to admire such wonders as the Great Sphinx at Giza and the giant pyramids.

Fava Beans

Fava beans, also known as broad beans, grow in pods, like peas. Fava beans must be shelled. The outer peel is tough. They must be cooked. Some people are allergic to raw fava beans. Fava beans come canned, dried, or frozen. Ful medames is made from cooked dried fava beans.

Cumin

The spice cumin is dried and ground from seeds of an herb related to parsley. Cumin is ancient. The spice has been found in the tombs of Pharaohs. It is used a lot in Mexican, Vietnamese, Thai, and Indian food.

whole cumin

ground cumin

What You Need

Equipment:

soup pot or frying pan

stirring spoon

Optional: potato masher

Ingredients:

1 can fava beans

1 teaspoon salt

sprinkle of black pepper

1 teaspoon cumin

1 clove crushed or minced garlic

1 tablespoon olive oil

1 tablespoon lemon juice (or lime juice)

pita

What's This?

The word "pita" (PEE-tuh) means bread in Aramaic, an ancient Middle Eastern language. Don't say "pita bread." That's like saying it twice!

Optional:

Top with diced tomato, diced onions or scallions, chopped fresh parsley, or cilantro.

Season with 1 teaspoon paprika, ½ teaspoon coriander, or a dash of cayenne pepper.

What to Do

1. Heat the fava beans in the pan.
2. Add salt, pepper, cumin, and garlic.
3. Simmer the fava beans for at least ten minutes, longer if you want. Leave the beans whole or crush them with a fork or potato masher.
4. Drizzle olive oil and lemon into the beans.
5. Serve hot with pita.

Serves 4.

Chapter 4

Khichadi

Khichadi (KITCH-uh-dee) is simple and bland. Rice and lentils are cooked until they are soft and creamy. Khichadi (also called khichari) is India's comfort food. It is easy to cook, a popular "campfire" food, and often the first solid food that babies in India eat.

India

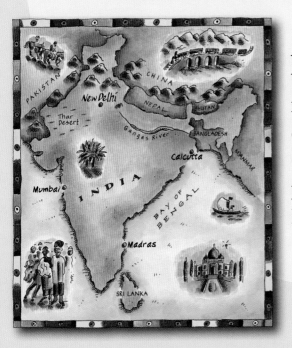

Although India is only one third the size of the United States, it is the second most populated country in the world (behind China), with over one billion people. India is also one of the largest countries in area.

Ghee

Ghee is made from butter that has been simmered to separate it into parts. Three layers form: water on top, butter in the middle, and milk solids on the bottom. The golden butter in the middle is ghee. Ghee does not burn when melted, like butter can.

What You Need

Equipment:

Heavy-bottomed soup pot with a lid

Strainer

Ingredients:

1 cup yellow lentils (also known as yellow moong dal)

4 cups of water + water for soaking

1 cup white basmati rice

1 teaspoon salt

½–1 teaspoon dried cumin

1 tablespoon ghee or olive oil

Optional: coriander; plain yogurt

What's This?

Basmati rice is grown in the Himalayas and Pakistan. When cooked, the long grains are fluffy, not sticky. Basmati has a delicate fragrance.

What's This?

Lentils are dried beans. They look like peas. Yellow lentils are softer than brown or green lentils.

What to Do

1. Rinse and drain the lentils.
2. To soak the lentils: Place in the pot. Cover with water. Heat to boiling. Turn off the burner, cover the pot, and let the lentils sit for two hours. Throw away any lentils that float on top. Drain the water.
3. Add 4 cups fresh water to lentils. Heat to boiling.
4. Add rice.
5. Add salt, cumin, and ghee or oil.
6. Stir.
7. Return to boil.
8. Lower the heat to low simmer. Cover the pot. Cook until the rice is soft and lentils are creamy and tender—about 20 minutes.

Serves 4 people.

Serve khichadi warm in bowls. Add salt and pepper to taste and an extra dab of butter if desired. If you like, sprinkle with coriander or add a spoonful of plain yogurt.

Cook's Tip

Soaking makes dried beans softer to lessen the cooking time. Some cooks skip soaking and just cook beans longer.

Cook's Tip

If your khichadi is too dry, add more boiling water. If it is too watery, simmer longer with the lid slightly off.

Chapter 5

Pannukakku

Pannukakku (BUNN-ew-guck-ew) is a baked pancake that is made with eggs. Pannukakku puffs up in the oven. It sinks as it cools. It is crusty on top but gooey inside, like custard. Pannukakku is sliced and served with fresh fruit, whipped cream, and powdered sugar.

Finland

Finland is a Scandinavian country. It is bordered by Sweden, Russia, and Norway. The capital, Helsinki, in southern Finland, is Europe's most northern capital city.

Lapland, Finland's northern province, is above the Arctic Circle. In the summer, the sun never sets. In the winter, the sun never rises. Some Laplanders herd reindeer.

Custard

Custard is made of eggs, milk and flour. Custard dates to the Middle Ages. Romans knew that eggs make ingredients stick together. Custard can be boiled, steamed, or baked. Britain is famous for its custardy Yorkshire pudding and popovers. Flan is a popular custard from Spain.

What You Need

Equipment:

Baking dish—deep oven-proof frying pan (not Teflon; check with a parent to make sure the dish is okay), pie plate, or 9x9 square baking dish

Bowl

Whisk

Oven mitts or pot holders

Spatula

Ingredients:

4 tablespoons butter

4 eggs

$\frac{1}{3}$ cup sugar

1 teaspoon vanilla

$\frac{1}{2}$ teaspoon salt

1 cup flour

2 cups milk

What to Do

1. Preheat the oven to 400 degrees.
2. Place butter in the baking dish.
3. Put the baking dish in the oven. It will heat up while you make the batter.
4. Beat the eggs. Add sugar, vanilla, and salt. Beat some more.
5. Add flour and milk alternately. ◀·····
6. Using oven mitts or pot holders, remove the baking dish from the oven.
7. With a spatula, spread the melted butter in the baking dish.
8. Pour batter into the baking dish. Scrape the bowl with a rubber spatula.
9. Return the dish to the oven.
10. Bake for 20 minutes.
11. Pannukakku will be golden brown. Take it out of the oven. Let it rest for 2 minutes or more.

Serves 2–4 people.

Slice and serve pannukakku warm. Choose your toppings—fresh berries or jam, whipped cream and powdered sugar, or maple syrup. Add a sprinkle of cinnamon or chocolate powder.

·····**What's This?**

Add some milk. Stir. Add some flour. Stir. Repeat three or four times until you've mixed in all the flour and milk.

Cook's Tip

Pannukakku puffs up. The batter should only come half-way up the sides of your baking pan. Otherwise it will spill over in the oven.

Cook's Tip

In the oven, place a cookie sheet on the oven rack below to catch butter drippings.

Chapter 6

Kielbasa and Toast

Polish people eat kielbasa (keel-BAH-suh) for breakfast, lunch, or supper, and with fried onions, horseradish, or mustard. Kielbasa is a kind of sausage. It is cooked in soup, beans, stew, dumplings, and sauerkraut.

Poland

Poland is a large country in central Europe. Its capital is Warsaw.

Poland's most famous musical composer was Frederick Chopin, who lived from 1810 to 1849. In good weather, 1,500 tourists visit his childhood home daily.

Kielbasa

In Polish, the word kielbasa (keel-BAH-suh) means sausage, any kind of sausage. Polish smoked kielbasa is made from ground pork, salt, pepper, and garlic. In the United States, many Polish delicatessens sell authentic smoked kielbasa.

What You Need

Equipment:
Frying pan and lid

Tongs

Toaster

Knife

Serving plate

Ingredients:
Water

Kielbasa

4 slices fresh dark bread—rye, pumpernickel, or wheat

Butter

Mustard

What's This?

Pinch tongs together to pick up or turn a piece of food.

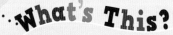

Cook's Tip

Find a fully-cooked kielbasa in the grocery store deli cooler. It will be near cooked meats like bratwursts, hot dogs, and ham.

What to Do

1. Pour a ½ inch layer of water into a frying pan.
2. With tongs, place the kielbasa in the pan on the stove.
3. Heat on medium-high until the water boils.
4. Lower the heat. Cover the pan.
5. Simmer 10 minutes, until most of the water is gone.
6. Toast and butter the bread.
7. Brown the kielbasa. Turn the heat up. Cook sausage for one minute on each side.
8. Place hot kielbasa on a serving plate. Slice it.
9. Eat it on toast with a dab of your favorite mustard.

Serves 4 people.

What's This?

Simmer means to steam at a low heat, just below the boiling point.

Cook's Tip

To "brown" means to darken the color. Browning kielbasa seals in juices and flavor and makes the outside crispy.

Fresh Fruit

Brazil is one of the world's largest producers of fresh fruit. Brazil exports grapes, melons, mangoes, apples, limes, bananas, papayas and many other fruits, like guava, cashew fruit, and passion fruit.

Brazil

Brazil is the largest country in South America. It's climate is tropical (hot and rainy). Over half of the Amazon rainforest is in Brazil. City streets in Brazil have many fruit markets and fresh juice bars. One popular fruit drink is pineapple blended with fresh mint leaves.

32

Pineapple

Pineapples are prickly. In Brazilian Portuguese, one word for pineapple is **abacaxi**. It means "stinking fruit." The word **abacaxi** also describes situations that are a total mess. The English word "pineapple" is an early version of "pine cone."

What You Need

mango

passion fruit

Equipment:
Cutting board

Sharp knife

Mango—Peel skin. Remove the large single seed

Passion fruit—Purple and wrinkly when ripe; seeds are edible.

Ingredients:
Choose fresh raw fruit:
Papaya—Yellow; soft when ripe. Peel off the skin and take out the seeds.

Guava—Small and round with white, pink, or red flesh. Edible skin and seeds

guava

Pineapple—Tough and prickly outside with edible fruit on the inside.

pineapple

papaya

What to Do

1. Peel and slice the fruits.
2. Squeeze a little lime or lemon juice over the fruit.
3. Cut the fruits into bite-sized chunks and mix for a fruit salad.
4. Eat!

Cook's Tip

To add protein, eat with nuts, cottage cheese, or yogurt.

Pineapple Mint Juice

In a blender, place:

1. 2 thick slices of fresh pineapple, peeled and cored, cut into chunks.
2. 1 glass cold water
3. fresh mint leaves, as many or few as you wish
4. a few ice cubes
5. 1 tablespoon sugar—more or less, to taste
6. Optional: ½ cup of orange juice
7. Blend until frothy and smooth. (Get an adult's help with this step.)

Serves 1 person.

This is a great drink on a hot summer day with a sandwich!

What's This?

Peel means to remove outer peel, rind, or skin. Core means to cut out the hard center.

What's This?

Find fresh mint in the grocery store or, in the summer, at a farmer's market. Plant mint in your garden—but be warned: Mint is a hardy plant. It will spread!

Chapter 8

Googs and Soldiers

"Googs and Soldiers" is Australian slang for fried eggs and toast. Australians reveal their sense of humor and love of language through slang. Cotton candy is called *fairy floss*. Hamburgers are grilled on the *barbie*, short for barbecue grill. Biscuits are *bikkies*. Candies are *lollies*. Breakfast is *brekkie*.

When you make this recipe, you can say, "How about googs and soldiers for brekkie, mate?"

Australia

Australia, which is the smallest continent, is located southeast of Asia. Sydney is the capital city of Australia. Australia is home to many exotic animals—such as kangaroos and koalas.

Eggs

The eggs people eat most come from chickens (though we can also eat duck eggs, pigeon eggs, and even ostrich eggs). Chickens in the United States produce 75 billion eggs a year. But that is only 10 percent of the world's egg supply!

What You Need

Equipment:
Frying pan
Spatula
Toaster
Serrated knife

Ingredients:
Eggs
Bread
Butter
Salt and pepper

Cook's Tip

Use 1–2 eggs and 1–2 slices of bread per person.

What's This?

A serrated knife has ridges or "teeth." It can cut soft food, like bread, pound cake, or tomatoes without squishing it.

What to Do

Fry the egg:

1. Heat the frying pan. Add a little butter to the pan.
2. Crack the egg into the melted butter in the pan.
3. You can either make the egg sunny side up or over easy. For sunny-side up—splash a tablespoon of water into the pan and cover to steam the egg. For over-easy—flip the egg gently with a spatula so it cooks on both sides.

Make toast:

1. Toast the bread in a toaster.
2. Butter the toast.
3. With the serrated knife, cut each piece of bread into three or four strips.

Place the eggs and toast together on a plate. Salt and pepper the egg to taste. Enjoy!

Serves 1 person.

Cook's Tip

Do you like the yolk runny or hard? The longer eggs cook, the harder the yolks get.

La Bouillie

La Bouillie (lah boo-EE-lee) is hot cereal from the African country of Chad. It is made with rice, millet, and peanut butter and served with milk and sugar, like oatmeal.

Chad

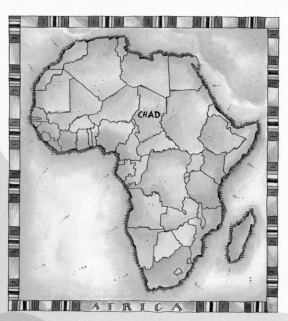

Chad is south of Libya, in central Africa. It is 3 times the size of California. It is landlocked–that means it has no borders on the sea. N'Dajamena is Chad's capital and largest city. Meat, fish, and cotton are Chad's most important products. People in Chad speak French or Arabic.

Millet

Millet is a grain. Millet grows in hot, dry fields. It is an important crop and a main food in Africa. It has been eaten as cereal in Africa for thousands of years.

What You Need

Cook's Tip

Not sure you will like a recipe? Make a smaller portion to try it out! Divide the amount of each ingredient in half.

Ingredients:

1 cup of cooked rice

1 tablespoon peanut butter

¼ cup wheat or millet cereal (optional)

½ cup milk

1 teaspoon sugar

Cook's Tip

This is a good way to use up leftover rice

Equipment:

Cereal bowl

Spoon

Microwave OR saucepan

What to Do

In the microwave:

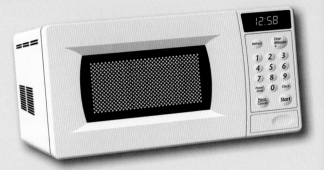

1. In a cereal bowl, mix all ingredients.
2. Heat in microwave for 30 seconds.
3. Stir until peanut butter dissolves.
4. Heat again in microwave until hot, about 45 seconds.

   OR

On top of the stove:

1. Mix all ingredients in a saucepan on the stove on low heat.
2. Stir until heated throughly.
3. Pour into a bowl.

Serves one.

Chapter 10
Coconut Syrup

In the United States, maple syrup is common on pancakes. In Jamaica, coconut is popular on almost everything. Next time you want pancakes, try making coconut syrup. Use it on waffles or French toast too, or put it on granola or fresh fruit. It's also good on chocolate ice cream!

Jamaica

Jamaica is a Caribbean Sea island in the Greater Antilles. The capital of Jamaica is Kingston. In Jamaica, the weather is sunny and warm (around 80 degrees) every day, with short rain showers.

41

Coconuts

Coconuts are round and hairy with hard shells. They look like big nuts but they are really fruits. Coconut palm trees can grow to be 90 feet tall. Each tree can make 75 coconuts a year. Coconuts produce fruit, oil, juice, and milk.

What You Need

Equipment:
Saucepan
Stirring spoon

Ingredients:
½ can of coconut milk
2 teaspoons cornstarch
¾ cup light corn syrup
3 tablespoons white sugar

What's This?
Cornstarch is a white, tasteless powder similar to flour. It makes liquids like soups and sauces thicker.

Cook's Tip

Shake the can of coconut milk before you open it.

What To Do

1. Heat coconut milk in a saucepan over medium heat. Stir often.
2. Add cornstarch. Stir until it dissolves.
3. Stir in corn syrup and sugar.
4. Stir constantly.
5. As soon as the syrup starts to boil, turn off the heat.
6. Take the pan off the burner.

Serves 4 people.

Serve coconut syrup warm or cold. Store leftovers in a container in the refrigerator to use again.

Cook's Tip

Stir nonstop. This keeps it from burning and spilling over

Chapter 11

Anijsmelk and Hagelslag

Anijsmelk (AN-ice-melk) is warm milk flavored with aniseed. Hagelslag(HAH-ghull-slog) are chocolate sprinkles. In the Netherlands, Dutch people put hagelslag on bread.

The Netherlands

The Netherlands is a country in northwestern Europe that sits at or below sea level. Seawalls protect the land from flooding. Most people in the Netherlands are Dutch. Herring and smoked eel are special fish dishes that the Dutch enjoy. Edam and Gouda are Dutch cheeses.

Anise und Hagelslug

Anise (ANN-iss) is a spice that has a sweet licorice taste. It is used to flavor many dishes.

Hagelslag (HAH-ghull-slog) are chocolate sprinkles. The sprinkles look like icy hail. In Dutch, the word *hagel* means hail; *slag* means battle or scuffle. So *hagelslag* means a scuffle of hail.

Anise seeds

What You Need

Equipment:

Thick-bottomed soup pot

Stirring spoon

Strainer

Butter knife

Toaster

Ingredients:

1 cup milk

1 teaspoon anise seed

2 teaspoons sugar or honey

Bread

Butter

Chocolate sprinkles

Cook's Tip

A heavy pan keeps the milk from burning. If you don't have a heavy pan, turn the heat down a little and stir often!

What to Do

Milk:

1. Heat the milk in the pan on medium low.
2. Crush the anise seeds.
3. Stir in crushed anise and sugar or honey.
4. Stir occasionally until the milk just boils.
5. Pour the milk through a strainer into a mug.

Cook's Tip

Place the seeds in a recloseable plastic sandwich bag and smash them with a rolling pin or a heavy spoon. Crushing spice seeds releases their aroma.

What's This?

A wire strainer will catch the anise seeds.

What's This?

Careful! Milk burns easily. Stir it often. Don't let it overcook.

Toast:

1. Make toast.
2. Butter the toast.
3. Sprinkle with hagelslag. Enjoy with your anijsmelk!

Serves 1 person.

Further Reading

Books

D'Amico, Joan, and Karen Eich Drummond. *The Coming to America Cookbook: Delicious Recipes and Fascinating Stories from America's Many Cultures.* Hoboken, N.J.: Wiley, 2005.

de Mariaffi, Elisabeth. *Eat It Up! Lip-Smacking Recipes for Kids.* Toronto: Owlkids, 2009.

Dodge, Abigail Johnson. *Around the World Cookbook.* New York: DK Publishing, 2008.

Lagasse, Emeril. *Emeril's There's a Chef in My World!: Recipes That Take You Places.* New York: HarperCollins Publishers, 2006.

Wagner, Lisa. *Cool Sweets & Treats to Eat: Easy Recipes for Kids to Cook.* Edina, Minn.: ABDO Publishing Co., 2007.

Internet Addresses

Cookalotamus Kids
<http://www.cookalotamus.com/kids.html>

PBS Kids: Cafe Zoom
<http://pbskids.org/zoom/activities/cafe/>

Spatulatta.com
<http://www.spatulatta.com/>

Index